Tales found in a psych ward

Poems the write wrote in a psych ward

DEDICATED TO

My friends who saved me!
My friends who I went through hell for!

Trap

The Raven flew so much
Until he got shot
Caught and brought to a cage
His wings stripped
Doomed and wingless
Can't see hope
Lost in dreams

Forgotten

Friendless

Sadness

Souless

Brokeness

The echos

The cries

The fear

The dear

The re-new of the free dear

White Room

The white room
The doomed raven
Where is home
There is no sanity
Madness lurks
Deep in the room
Lurking hope
Laughing king
This king hurts
This king is hopeless

Forgotten II

The running
The lonliness
Do they care
Do they love
Do they run
Who is
Who was
Thanks
Pain

Doctor and Pacient

The Doctor

The Pacient

Dripping pacience

Sandman oh sandman

Take me to my dreams

Don't bring me back

For I am homeless in a timeless prison

Mind State

The empty place
When laughter is
Where joy was
Where depair was
Where blank is
Will I ever break free?
For this constant
Constant screams
Constant emotions
Constant hopeless
Won't stop
I AM HELPLESS

Caged Love-thoughts

Who would love

A patient

A person

As broken as me

As time passes

I have no motion

I have no wings

I am unlovable

Tick tock

The clock goes

The hand spins

For no time passes

In this hellish place

Hole of the Mole

Hole
Whole
Fill the whole
Fill it whole
For my hole is huge
A mole burrows around
Eating it whole
This mole is loneliness
The mole who opens
the hole in my heart

Knocking On My Mind's Door

Knock.

Knock?

Knock!

Who's there?

Sandman

Who?

I am coming to help.

Help?

I thy sandman will take you to your dream as you wish

Rustmaton

Rusty Automaton
No parts
Only Cranks
No heart
More Empty than a Can
No Oil
No Gears
No one remembers him

Departed

A part

Alone

Missing ya'll

It hurts

It hurts

It sucks

To be apart of people

Can I heal

Can I deal with this

Deal damage

deal heal deal

Caged bird

The window

The Cage

The man

The raven

Looks out and Sees

Birds

Freedom

Looks in and sees

Fears

Doom

Far Kingdom

Far away

Four way

Forwards

To the kingdom

Step back

Lack the will

The will to go to the kingdom

The kingdom of dreams

Nail

Nail to the coffin
Bail me out
Knock open this place
Chased from home
To this place
Rock is stuck
Rock is heart
This heart of stone
Makes my bone break
Makes my muscles shake
Atone from your emotions

Admission

Wednesday black
Crack my brain
Wednesday blue
I was subdue
Wednesday tears
Stares my past
Wednesday Glitch
Snitch I am safe
Wednesday stain
I am in pain

Guard

The guard of the heart ward
Has fallen
The forgotten and the rotten
Faulty human
Will he be saved
Will he be slayed
Will he be forgotten

Friday Joy

It's Friday
Birds are blooming
Flowers are singing
Stars are crying
Babies are shining
On days like this
Kids like me
Should be flying away

Flight Lights

Should I take flight
Should I fight
Caught and flapping his wings
A light
A bright fright
Write or Die
Miss or be Missed
Cry or Laugh
Kiss or Rip

Shaved Raven

They shaven the Raven

They engraven the white out

The white raven

He was frighten

They fight him with sheer emotions

Fear he felt

Reaper he wished

Hope he saught

Dove of Love

The dove carries love
The raven carries craving
The raven loves
The Dove falls
The white raven takes flight
Only to crash
What a trash

Happiness

Happy Pill
Kill my sadness
Rise my Badies
What's Happiness
What's Freedom
That undying bloom
That creeping doom
The ending riff
Down the cliff

Big Heart

A bad heart
A sad soul
Heave my heart
Weave my soul
Depart away
Slay thy life
For I arise
No more cries
Lie down
Rest upon the ravens nest

Eeek

Scratching Sound
Scratches in my soul
Scratches on the wall
Screaming out
Let them out
My feelings
My emotions
My metal heart
Art is fire
Art is freedom
Art breaks through

2 Hell and back

Ride with Friends
Follow them
Would you ride
To find yourself
To find them
Hello wake up
You are fight for thy friends
Heal my soul
So I can be with my friends
I'd go to this hellish place
I'd conquer death
I'd conquer dreams
And got out of here FOR MY FRIENDS

Metal IS METAL

The metal
In the mental ward
Rages my soul
Moves my strings
Stings my Crown
Down with the King
My mental breakdown
For I am mentally METAL!

Flowers & Bell

Flowers growing of the bell towers
Seeking the power
Flowing vines
Shines like the sun
The old bell tower
The gold rust shining
Gust and Dust
Scraping the Bell

Prison Son

Prison son cry
Son is locked up in prison
A medical prison
1 week
I am weak
The peak
Don't peek
Don't squeak
For you're a son in prison
Stuck up
Suck it up

Mind Battery

1 percent battery of the factory
Ready for a breakdown
Ready for a forest fire
Blood pouring down natures wrist
Humans sawing down wood
Nature saws down mans bones
Mentally unstable runes
Written in this walls
Tear them down
Like this prison and this mental ward
This is my nature

Conjuror of Dreams

Warlock conjuror of dreams

Lock my dreams

Throw the key

Let me out

From nightmare

I'm a mere mortal

A mere poet

Seeking a maiden

Seeking a poem

Seeking a way out

Drive away

Loud and Clear

Shout out loud

A load of nonsense

Shout out

Doubts and Fear

A teddy bear

A care package

Throw everything

Deeping fear

Dear dreamer

Shout

Screech

There is no ecape from this nightmare

Insane

Insane in here

Same out there

Lane of dreams

Dreamers are like Drummers

Hitting

Hurting

Raging

Breaking in

Out of here

Won't work

Stay 1 week

Suffer 1 week

The wall

The wall is stronger than diamonds
Unattracted to anyone yet powerful
Mentally unstable emotions in love with the wall
Only to get crushed
Only to crash strainght into
Luckily he survived
Mentally unstable at the ward
Recovering from the crash
trying to understand his love and dreams
Such a daredevil
Strucked by a devil
To crash to a wall

Waves

Mood waves
Heart beats
Broken vases
Lost at sea
Ghost of me
Host a boast
The waves are still
Due to the conquerer
Stabilizer of waves
A Pill calmer
A happy pill
Set me free
From the warm sunset
Take me to the night
Where the light of the moon calls for me

Timeless Zone

Time?
Where are you?
Where am I?
Prison?
Ward?
Definetly a psych ward
No screams. Quiet
Peaceful although brutal
Wizard wand can't heal me
Wizard potion weakenss me
Blue meds
Blue pill
Green bill
Hurtful

Bard Song #1

A song from a bard

Hard feelings comeout

A harp of soothing sounds

Howling hound

Howling anger

Soothing angel

Come to me

Sing to me

Like a Bard's song

Mother's Love

Mother Loves Me
A tad too much
Others love
Not too much
Robot feelings
Missing emotions
Doing okay
Loving badly
Wishing harder
To be set free

Thinking...

Thinking
King of my live
King of my soul
Lovers and past Lovers
Come and go
But all is over
After I hurt you
I'm under dirt
Thinking of life
Holding a Knife
To cut off my mistakes
Please accept me

Mind Hive

Mind hive
Where thoughts live
They come alive
From emotions to dreams to nightmares
No motion scared me
There is constant shock everywhere
Beams of fear struck my brain
Bring me life
Rings of mood
Tell me the mood
Hidden by my heart

Puppet Strings

Puppet strings

Guitar strings

Riffing away stings my fingers

Each string tells a story

One tells about the puppet

And one of a metal bucket
But all are heavy metal

Metal issues are fixed by a blacksmith

Mental issues engraved by a Doctor

Post Apocalyptic

Trumpet

Sounds

Drunk

Unhealed Wounds

The foaming mouth of a hound
The bitten wound
Opened again so I can claen
Maggots coming from within
Rotten wound
Amputate my flesh
Forgotten Damage
This rash in my brain
Rip this pain away
Pray for my Survival
Fray my skin
Slough my emotions

Uncaged

Open the cage
Let love out
Let dove out
Flying away from you
Say I don't want you fool
Slay the love of this fool
I am not a tool for this foolishness
I am but a sire
Who wears the tire crown
Caster of fire and chaos
I shall rise up
I shall rinse the tears
I shall cut the pain
But not in vain

God where r u?

God are you here?
Here in this place?
All I want is freedom
Take my soul from this kingdom
Free me
I need to flee
I need you
You freed me before
From Greed
From sadness
From madness
My highness thanks

Neit

At night Neit requests worship
The Knight calls forth Neit
To sink the warship
Neit draws his sword
The warship starts to fire
Neit conceal his sword
The warship falls
Seal your war
Thall shall not fight
When the night come
When the knight cry
Fight or Love
Fighting passion
Fearsome position

Too bright

Lower the brightness of my life
Let the darkness out
God savior of my darkness
God over darkness
Worship God
This warship is painted black
Need a needle from a haystack
To sow my stitches
No more sorrow
My savior has risen
Conquerer of death
Conquerer of my life
I kneel before you

Window

Windows seprates our world
Old men built those windows
I see birds flying time passing
I imagine a sea of freedom
Calling upon this day
As the sun stops shining
I a son cries for no time
As the moon rises
Sad man loan no dreams
But they hope for better days
Hopes for life
Hopes for mirrored evil
Which is life in its purest

Sheer Heart of Fear

Sheer the fear of the shire
Dire hope
For to be a squire
Liar to the truth
Seeker of the truth
Creature of madness
For to be a squire
Liar to the truth
Seeker of truth
Creature of truth
Foaming Fearfulness
I shall slay the creature
For I am the knight
For I am the night
Good Night

Double Faced

Two faced
The poet
The puppet
The poet writes
The puppet cries
The poet pulls the strings
The puppet reads the strings
The poet reads the strings
The poet dreads his life
The puppet drives for life
The poet wants a wife
The puppet wants life
They live in the same body

Timey Whining

To turn back time
To save my younger self
To a prime time
So I won't be slave to pain
Sour lime of life
Can't you be less bitter sweet
Chugging beer won't solve sorrows
Take a dive through time
All the holes I burrow though
All the pain I see
I want to flee this sour moments
So I can have a sorrow free life

Anxiety Sonnet

Prison thoughts crossing my mind in shackles
Insanity thoughts speeding through my mind
Arisen from my grave and crawl away
The profanity forming from my mind
Rush of feeling making me nests all around
Anxiety calling Flight or Fight
Gush of emotions forming from chipping
The shackles of sanity piercing skin
I'm not insane like others in here
To be normal what is it anyways
The bane of my mind due to you, brother
You informal fool slay the beast within
Psycho overkilling emotions
Maestro has the emotions screeching, please

The pressure of the beast

Each step I take
It creeps in
The footsteps grow louder
The growls of the beast
Become louder
Become stronger
Your heart start to thump
You bump into it
The growls turn into cries
For this is depression

Conquerer

Walk tall

Fly like a Hawk

Cry over nothing

Coughing thoughts

Astronauts of the S P A C E

Have they reached base?
Conquerer of planets comeback

Have you planed your next move

Dreams aren't for sleep deprived

King over Darkness

Lethal pain
Metal fire
Chain the devil down
King over darkness
In midnight he raises stars
Light the way
In doubts pray
In a tight knot PRAY
No more darkness
Raise the cross
He died and came back!

No control

Sorry I write poetry
Sorry I write emotions
Sorry if I write about you
Ivory woods I miss them
Can I ORA like Jotaro's stand
Punch wood like Saitama
Pull a rasengun like Naruto
No I'm a mere mortal
I dare you to forgive me
Guns won't solve anything
Cuz you didn't give me a shot

Squeak isn't Speak

How to Speak
All that comes is squeak
How to say my conclusion
Is it disillusion
Take my love away from me
Did I feel like a locked dove?
I missed that feeling
That rush of something
Brush this because you ain't my lover
Sorry I see now all that pain
Nothing was invain you are my best friend
Not a lover more like a friend I care for

Rainbowie

Love has many colors
Friendship is one color
Warmth, light, happy
Lover is two colors
Lover is toxic, Lover is Warmth
But don't mix them
For they don't wan't to look gray
For you'll get confused
Fix them by learning to differentiate
Learn to pay well for them
Growth is needed

Cups

Curse to find love
What is Love for me
A forbidden verse of desire
Kind of a complex feeling
Is love toxic?
The only time I tasted
I drank from the wrong cup
At bedtime I pounder about the right cup
I was eaten up and thrown away
I miss that rush
I miss those feelings
I don't miss her!
I wish you the best wrong cup!

Where r u?

God isn't in darkness thy say
He dwells in darkness for the broken I say
He has spoken light in darkness
Can't fear darkness without the hope for light
I dwell in darkness in search of light
My darkness is not more for he has risen

Female Doggo

She rocked in red
Her black hair entangled my heart
Tore my heart to shreds
1000 volts of toxic shock
Pain is just a feeling
Tingling emotions you made me insane
Stuck in a prison cell
Sucking my thumb like a baby
Don't come closer
Don't see me ever again
Sayonara cold female dog

Plague

Doctor are you here to take me
Doctor don't you shock me
Doctor shocked me
Doctor mocked me
Doctor don't make me go
Plague I ain't got one
Your crow mask scares me
This green glow are you a ghost
Below the depths you wait
Is this my fate as a fallen soul
At this rate I've given up

The Four Horsemen Nursery

The four Horsemen rule over land
Conquest is conquering fast faster
War is warring hard and harder
Famine is famishing strong and stronger
Death is collecting souls more and more
Don't fear their horses
Their forces bring a end
The horseman are coming
Don't run away

In path

Empath soul
Like a sponge
Emotions path it's way to you
Run away haven't you thought?
Misbehave is no option
Have you thought of peace
Haven't seeked pain for a while
It runs to me
From all those leaky people

Emotions Adrenaline

The constant hiding
The constant running
Where will this end
Here I stand
My fears don't end and don't grow
This glow on my emotions
They grow stronger of being below

Spree

Poetry spree

Poet emotions are sucked

Free the poet he hails you a lot

Tired from thinking

He hails poetry

He fails with rhymes

He bails from writing

He rests from constant torment

Journal

Oh journal, my Journal
My mind is your's
Feel's more like a rental
Don't bind my mental state into you
State the pain and write
Break the boundries of okay and ok
Ties from the past won't affect me
Last time you made me cry
Please no more cries from you
I love you my journal
I crave my poetry
Thanks for being here

Poetic Poetry

Did I fall in love with poetry
But poetry is me
All the time I saw poetry as a woman
Poetry is a man because poetry is me
As I juggle words
It becomes me
It becomes poetry
I don't struggle I write
I create stories with me
To tell a story
Same as claiming glory
I love poetry

Voice

My own voice
Is my word choice in each poem
English is my throne
Wish you could see my mind
I bind words into paper
Cower for my power over poems
Words are my secret power
Don't lower the curtains
This is just the beginning
The show musn't stop

Panic

Screams around me
Are driving me
A kid with no ice cream
Bound this person down
Her stress is stressing me
Pressing under pressure
Sure you might be right
A poet needs peace right?
At least the white raven wants.

Anger

Anger burdens me
Bridge my emotions
Bringer of rage
Slaying the roar of lions
A eon ago he arose
Fear the anger
Bringer of rage and death
Can't slay him

Brain Fart

Racing a motorcycle on a bicycle

Can't imagine winning

Leap for joy

Motorcycle ran off with fear

Bicycle ran off with determination

The nation cheers for the bicycle

Cycling away

Fear not a horse enters

No winner

Horse got tired

Bike got a flat tire

Motorcycle lost a tire

Writing and... Writing!

Keep writing
The poet says
No resting for his mind
Pulling thoughts from the closet
Burning brain
Forcing emotions my hand can't handle
Blow the candle and free me
Flee from my thoughts!
I bound my thoughts to paper
I scream a loud for freedom

Wizard x Poet

The poet wears a mask
The wizard wears a robe
The poet brings a flask of the past
The poet spins the globe the world spins
The wizard casts a spell
The poet yells to his spell
The place dim a battle of wizards and poets
The wizard casts his words
The poet binds the wizard's words
The wizard blinds himself
The poet outlasts the wizard
The wizards draws his wand
The poet throws his word
Binding the blind wizard on paper

Sailing to hell and heaven

I sail through hell on a tiny boat
I yell I'll be back as the gates close
The head of a huge goat shines ahead
Rise my son God calls me
I sail through heaven
When will this journey end?
Tomorrow a great end will come
There will be fights and cheers
I'll kill my past
I'll flight back to my friends
Two cups of Ginger beer
Will I be happy once again?

Block? Unblock!

Writer block
Poets cry
Focus too much on black
Carry a burden
I blank the mind
Loosen thy self
Bind your thoughts
On paper shelves
Stack them up
Don't slack
Don't doubt yourself
Write and write
Until thy die

Carpe Diem

Carpe Diem
Pluck the strings
Pluck the day
Seize it
For the future is a far
For the present is here
Cure the present
Future in development
Carpe Diem
Screw the future
I'm in the presnt

Hellway the psych ward

Hell is a one way down
Hallways are straight and empty
This timeless place
A plane of reality closest to hell
Is this Hellway this timeless Hellway
Safety check
Fear check
Fake smiles check
Welcome to my personal hell
Welcome to the timeless Hellway

Timeless paradise

Timeless paradise
No time
Just rhymes
There is a clock
We are a lock away
In sock we slide
Blockout of reality
This is life in hallway
All the way
This ain't paradise

Tomorrow

Tomorrow smells better

I want to bite the marrow of better days

Will there be freedom or inprison tomorrow

My wish of freedom

My fear of imprison

Sleep for tomorrow will be the present

Bite the marrow of your dreams

Stranger

Stranger Roommate
Danger is ticking in my brain
Who is this man
My heart is in pain because of anxiety
Darts straight to my heart
They tell me to run
They tell me to hide
What if he is a nice dude

Train

Chu chu the screams of the train
Nailing my brain down
Chu chu off the trails of my mind
Trail of forest I'm lost in my mind
Chu chu off the rails
Tied to the rails
This train is going to run over me
Chu chu chu

Ghosts

My day's in this Hellway will be black
I've paid my way
I've paid my lack of faith
Free me I ain't no goon
I want be gone from this hell
I yell let me out
This wraith in this place
Smells like ghosts